THIS BOOK
BELONGS TO

....

....

Thank you for Purchasing my book and taking the time to read it from front to back. I am always grateful when a reader chooses my work and I hope you enjoyed it!

With the vast selection available online, I am touched that you chose to be purchasing my work and take valuable time out of your life to read it. My hope is that you feel you made the right decision.

I very much would like to know what you thought of the book. Please take the time to write an honest and informative review on Amazon.com. Your experience and opinions will be of great benefit to me and those readers looking to make an informed choice.

With much thanks.

@COPYRIGHT 2024

The content contained within this book may not be reproduced, duplicated, or transmitted without direct written permission from the author or the publisher. Under no circumstances will any blame or legal responsibility be held against the publisher, or author, for any damages, reparation, or monetary loss due to the information contained within this book. Either directly or indirectly.

Legal Notice:

This book is copyright protected. This book is only for personal use. You cannot amend, distribute, sell, use, quote, or paraphrase any part, or the content within this book, without the consent of the author or publisher.

Disclaimer Notice:

Please note the information contained within this document is for educational and entertainment purposes only. All effort has been executed to present accurate, up-to-date, and reliable, complete information. No warranties of any kind are declared or implied. Readers acknowledge that the author is not engaging in the rendering of legal, financial, medical, or professional advice. The content within this book has been derived from various sources. Please consult a licensed professional before attempting any techniques outlined in this book. By reading this document, the reader agrees that under no circumstances is the author responsible for any losses, direct or indirect, which are incurred as a result of the use of the information contained within this document, including, but not limited to — errors, omissions, or inaccuracies.

Table of Contents

OK—What's Fine Doing	5
Lesson 1: OK to take your time	6
Lesson 2: OK to be jealous	10
Lesson 3: OK to lose	13
Do—What You Should Be Doing	16
Lesson 4: Do start selling	17
Lesson 5: Do stretch yourself early	20
Lesson 6: Do think in terms of your values	23
Lesson 7: Do exercise prudence	26
Lesson 8: Do select your friends	29
Don't—What You Shouldn't Be Doing	32
Lesson 9: Don't just listen	33
Lesson 10: Don't let money be your goal	36
Lesson 11: Don't let others define your worth	40
Lesson 12: Don't find rich friends	43
Lesson 13: Don't be on my side	45
Lesson 14: Don't take anything for granted	47
Lesson 15: Don't neglect your health	50
Lesson 16: Don't expect others to change	52

OK—What's Fine Doing

LESSON 1

OK to take your time

Son, as you advance through your school years and get your first job, you'll quickly come to realize that many people are sprinting at a pace that is unsustainable through the rest of their careers. They want to get the next promotion as soon as possible, they'd like to be the youngest partner at the firm, and so forth. It's good that they try hard and give it their best, and I sincerely hope those are some of the values you embody as well. However, you need to realize that life is a marathon and not a sprint. Those one or two years of accelerated advancements don't necessarily mean anything in the long run, especially if the job you're in doesn't sync with your long-term career goals. So, don't be disappointed or demotivated if others seem to be progressing more rapidly than you. Instead, find what you truly want and give it your best to learn as much as possible, and the results will surely follow.

When I went to elementary school in Germany, the school decided to advance me to the next grade because I was better in all subjects than my peers of the same age. For the first time in the school's history, they held a teacher's conference to discuss whether to have me skip a grade and collectively decided to permit that. My parents were extremely excited to hear the news as for them it meant that I was smarter than others (and that's music to any parent's ears), though that one year of advancement truly didn't matter much in the end. When my family moved back to South Korea several years later, the school preferred I'd be placed into my original grade given my Korean language skills weren't on par with others and they thought it was against the norms to accept someone who was a year younger than the classmates. So, everything reversed itself and I technically repeated a year of sixth grade, which in fact, wasn't a bad experience at all—I had the time to hone my language skills, was able to familiarize myself with the culture and befriend peers of my same age, before advancing to middle school.

I've interviewed many candidates for investment banking analyst and associate positions who had decided to take some time off before they graduated to explore an internship, start a business or even travel around the world. Those few months or sometimes a year may appear to be a "hole" on their resume at first glance, but if you learn from those endeavors and get even slightly closer to what you want to do in life, that's a huge success and not a failure. Many times, I've found that those candidates were able to explain why they were interested in investment banking more effectively than others that presumably just wanted to get into it because it was a sexy, rewarding career. And by the way, that extra year or so of work experience that your peers may have from joining an investment bank before you do, may appear to be huge and irreversible during the first year or two at work, but you'll quickly be able to catch up and even exceed them in performance if you put in the effort. So, don't simply follow others into thinking you should be doing certain things under a specific timeframe, as you're much better off exploring first what you'd like to do than doing things first and frequently changing paths. Of course, it's difficult to figure out what you'd like to do, and frankly, people at my age still struggle with it, but don't just go with the flow and follow everyone else because of peer pressure. I'd like for you to think as hard as possible (and take your time in doing so) to determine what you'd like to become, as that's what's important and not that extra year or two of experience or accelerated advancement.

A close friend of mine, Jason, started out in private equity and moved into management consulting soon after, as he couldn't resonate with his firm's investment thesis focused heavily on financial engineering and drastic cost reduction measures. When he joined consulting, he came in as a fresh business analyst (i.e., entry level position) and spent six years at the firm to then go after his MBA at INSEAD. Post business school, he spent the next five years at Samsung's technology innovation team and now is off to private equity again—this time, as a leadership position and with partners who share the same investment philosophy as he does. Jason previously told me that he was one of the oldest students among his peers during his MBA, so he would often wonder if his decision to pursue an advanced degree was the right one. Witnessing his peers from college advancing to senior manager positions, it simply wasn't easy for him to quit his job and start out fresh as an MBA candidate. But he did it anyways, took on the risk, welcomed the uncertainty, and followed his heart. Though it took him a while to figure out what he wanted to do, he has now found the place he wants to be in the long run, leading the investment in the U.S., Europe, and Southeast Asia. He couldn't be happier that he had made the switch despite some others belaboring his choices initially.

I myself wanted to get into Wall Street, so decided to spend two years in business school. Well, including the preparatory efforts of writing the essays, taking the GMAT, and going through interviews, the commitment was probably closer to three years. Having been a top performer at my prior consulting firm, the partners didn't want to lose me and thus entertained the idea of promoting me early to engagement manager if I stayed with the firm. They also discussed sponsoring my tuition if I decided to return to the firm post business school. Though these proposals were extremely enticing and gratifying to me, my passion for investment banking drew me away. Candidly, it wasn't just the passion, but my realization that I should be evaluating my career in the long term (versus short term gains) so I must do the things I like or else I wouldn't be happy or competitive. Imagine working on things that you don't necessarily enjoy very much while having a passion for something else—that's simply sad and unproductive, isn't it? You should pursue the things you'd like to do even if it takes time and effort to get there. And what's important in life is to first identify *what* to aim at and then determine *how* to get there (as opposed to vice versa), as you can't know how to get there if you don't even know where you're aiming at. Spinning the wheels without much of a direction is silly, but having a goal, whether vague or clear, and pushing to get there is so much more productive.

So, don't be shy or afraid in taking your time to explore things, see different perspectives, meet and interact with various people. Those are invaluable experiences that will shape your thinking and ultimately your goals and meaning of life. Don't feel obliged to follow the paths of others, but rather pursue what's meaningful to you. That will differentiate you from others, give you a competitive edge, and provide you with a sense of accomplishment.

LESSON 2

OK to be jealous

Son, I'm going to tell you in Lesson 16—"Don't expect others to change" that changing others is nearly impossible, and you should refrain from even trying that. But accomplishing anything else is in the realm of possibility as long as you have the strong desire and perseverance to pursue it, and there's some luck involved.

When I was in college, I wanted to get into management consulting to learn as much as possible in a short period of time. When I was in consulting, I wanted to get into business school to transition into M&A investment banking. I always had a passion for teaching and sharing my knowledge, so beginning this fall, I'll be teaching finance and valuation to graduate students at New York University as an adjunct professor. All of this may seem simple and easy in writing, but I put quite a bit of effort into each step. Let me briefly tell you how I secured the adjunct role at NYU.

Your mother and I were vacationing with Alan, my best friend in college, and his wife in 2017. Alan shared that he had become an adjunct in the dental school of a state university near his residence. I was happy for him, yet a sense of jealousy crossed my mind as teaching had been my passion for years. At that time, your mom was pursuing her master's degree in global affairs at NYU. Prompted by

Alan's accomplishment and knowing that I had always wanted to teach, I discussed with your mother the idea of whether it'd be possible for me to secure a position at NYU. She noted that several classmates had always complained that financial modeling skills were required when applying for jobs, regardless of whether those were finance positions. And that the global affairs program lacked the technical classes to support recruiting for such positions. Your mother took those findings to the academic director and began having casual discussions around adding a workshop to help students better equip themselves with technical skills. In parallel, I began attending mentoring nights to meet with the NYU faculty and students, get to know their interests, and understand the shortcomings of the curriculum. Having been in consulting and investment banking for ten years at this point, I felt very comfortable teaching finance. Our joint efforts ultimately boiled down to me hosting a workshop at NYU, teaching financial modeling and valuation for five or more hours on a sunny Saturday morning in 2019. I had prepared materials, practiced presenting them for several hours, and even developed workshop evaluation questionnaires to solicit feedback from students and pass those along to the academic director if favorable. Fortunately, the results of the surveys were phenomenal and not long after sending those to the academic director, I was sitting down with her to talk about what specifically I'd be teaching the following semester.

I'd like for you to remember that the global affairs program at NYU wasn't planning on hiring someone to teach finance and valuation. It was your mother and I that proactively explored and found the opportunity to teach a topic I was very comfortable teaching. Our sustained efforts to communicate with the faculty, identify the curriculum's shortcomings, and solicit the students' interests and needs were what had led to securing this role—teaching a full credit course to graduate students at an institution as highly regarded as NYU.

Another lesson here is to ask for what you want. If you don't ask, who will know or care to know what you want? If you do ask, the worst thing that can happen to you is to be ignored or neglected. When I was recruiting for consulting, I proactively reached out to my contacts and expressed my interest and qualifications to get into the field, which helped me secure an internship. When I wanted to get the adjunct role, I proved myself worthy of the role through the workshop and asked that they bring me in as an adjunct and make any necessary adjustments to the curriculum to accommodate. When you've finally found your significant other, you will be asking the big question—will you marry me? So, if you want things, ask. Silence and inaction are the silliest states to be in when you truly want something. As Bible verse Matthew 7:7 succinctly states: "Ask, and it will be given to you; seek and you will find; knock and the door will be opened to you."

Who knows where the future will take us. But the uncertainty is what excites me, and I look forward to making possible the things we thought weren't once possible. Don't confine yourself into thinking you should walk a certain path, as you can create and design your own path if none exists. If you're at a crossroads, remember that you can always ask for help.

LESSON 3

OK to lose

Son, you will win, you will lose, and sometimes you won't be able to tell the difference between the two until time has passed. Winning provides a sense of immediate satisfaction and accomplishment. Losing, on the other hand, is disappointing, painful, and sometimes even embarrassing at first sight. But losing reveals its true value when you're able to reflect on it and learn what you could do better next time you're faced with a similar situation.

I look back and realize I have experienced several significant losses (or they at least appeared to be losses at that time). When I was a Sergeant in the Army, I ran for a supervisor position, which oversaw all KATUSA (Korean Augmentation to the U.S. Army) soldiers in the camp I was stationed in. One other candidate competed with me for the same role. I was pretty sure I'd win given the counterpart wasn't necessarily liked by many soldiers, so I didn't put in the effort to market myself. When the results came out though, my votes only represented a third of the total. I was disappointed and confused, wondering how he had won by such a significant difference. It turned out that my competitor had made every effort to solicit votes, meeting with the soldiers including trainees and discussing his perspectives on changing irritating reporting systems, etc. Ever since then, I've realized that the remorse

I feel for not trying is much more painful than the actual work that goes into trying, and the learning that comes from trying was extremely rewarding. From this moment onwards, I got into the habit of always giving my best.

A year or so later, when I was a fresh business analyst at my former consulting firm, my inability to speak Korean fluently overwhelmed me. Consulting is a job of persuading clients with logical thoughts and words, so having only lived in Korea for a few years was detrimental. During a live engagement, my manager openly voiced his disappointment in my performance, specifically pointing out that he needed to correct my writing extensively. Knowing that I had been in the office late for several weeks, he asked that I go home to rest and return the next morning refreshed. Confused if this was a sign to terminate me or if he truly wanted me to get some rest, I obeyed and cautiously left the office. I remember taking the subway, getting home around 7 p.m. and showering under hot water, only to decide that I'd go back to the office and prove myself. An hour or so later, I arrived back at the site to find my manager still working on the presentation. With an astonished set of eyes, he asked: "Why are you here?" I said I was here to work and learn. He replied it wasn't necessary, but I stayed and requested that he send any prior presentations he had worked on so I could learn the professional language and the logical flow of thinking. I recall I was there well past midnight. But more importantly, I probably spent more than eighty percent of my free time over the next several months on combing through the presentations and learning the language/flow. Not meeting my manager's expectations was a huge loss for me, but pushing myself to be better was the lesson that changed my life. I subsequently ranked top tier for the next couple of years I was at the consulting firm.

Give everything you have, and you'll always be a true winner. Recognize that failure isn't about not accomplishing your established goals, but more about not growing and learning from your losses. Acknowledge that without suffering, the growth you'd like to see probably doesn't come along. And if you continue to be upset about a loss or failure, ask yourself whether you've already paid more than what it's worth to you.

Do—What You Should Be Doing

LESSON 4

Do start selling

Son, do you know why the iPhone sells well relative to other mobile devices? The specs on paper and pricing aren't what drive the sales. Let's quickly examine the specs of the latest and greatest releases from Apple and OnePlus—iPhone 11 Pro versus OnePlus 7 Pro. Though the iPhone was released four months after the OnePlus, it's nearly ten percent heavier, lags in display resolution, doesn't provide dual-SIM functionality in the U.S., has much slower charging capabilities, fewer megapixels on the front-facing camera, and is nearly double the price tag. So how come Apple's U.S. market share is forty-two percent in the third quarter of 2019 (according to Counterpoint) vis-à-vis OnePlus' relatively insignificant market position? Let's leave aside the operating systems and design, as those are subjective and vary considerably from person to person. I personally attribute the significant difference in sales to Apple's marketing efforts and brand value. Apple has established itself as a leading premium consumer electronics company, spending $1.8 billion in advertising in 2015 alone. Note that they stopped disclosing advertising spend after 2015, but you'll see that selling, general, and administrative expenses (which includes advertising spend) exceeded $4.4 billion in the third fiscal quarter of 2019 alone.

To put things into perspective, that amounts to more than a hundred thousand years of rent that we're currently paying!

The reason I brought up the Apple example is that I want you to know that marketing and selling yourself are extremely important as you advance through your career. I'll elaborate more on career progression in the next chapter, Lesson 5—"Do stretch yourself early," but what I want to highlight here is that you must be able to sell what you did, what you've accomplished, and what you're capable of doing in order to get full credit for the work. I'm not saying you should put others under the bus or show off your work in an arrogant manner, but I encourage you to find ways to underscore your contributions, as your managers often have no idea who did what, given how busy they are. Believe it or not, selling yourself is sometimes more important than the quality of work you produce, as apparent in the iPhone example I described above.

When I was a consultant in 2012, I drove the analysis of the Chinese logistics industry and competitive landscape for a leading global logistics company planning to enter the Chinese market. I was promoted in 2011, so I had been invited to participate in a global training program held in Prague, Czech Republic, a month or so after the consulting project had kicked off. Knowing the amount of work that still needed to be done ahead of the final report/presentation, I warily asked my director whether it'd be OK for me to attend the training. The director said, "Of course, don't worry about it and go, thanks for checking in," so I did. After coming back from the training session that lasted about a week, I returned to the client site and decided to grab coffee with the director to get the lowdown on how things had progressed. The first words that came out of his mouth were: "Soo Jin, I had no idea how much you had contributed to this project. You nearly did everything. So, when I had asked your colleagues to refine some analyses and the presentation, they indicated that you had been in the weeds and running workstreams to a point where it was difficult for them to make any type of adjustments." Being a very diligent guy, I had made sure I passed on everything to my colleagues ahead of my departure to training, but it seemingly wasn't enough given the amount of work that had already been done. I knew at that point that seniors don't necessarily know each individual's contribution and quality of work, so I had to ensure I proactively displayed, communicated, and marketed my contributions (which I never did throughout the course of the project) when the opportunity presented itself.

Similar situations occur in investment banking. The highest-paid bankers are typically those that persistently sell themselves and their contributions. Those who have done great work but are too shy/quiet to make themselves noticeable tend to be regarded as not having worked hard enough or unpresentable to clients, and thus suffer in the reviews. Modesty is a value that's embedded in me, but excessive modesty may harm you in your career, particularly if everyone else is selling their skills and contributions. Keep in mind that social norms and cultures determine what attributes are desirable in any given organization. In the U.S., you need to showcase your capabilities and contributions proactively. By comparison, being humble and modest will often be more respected in Korea. In the U.S., communicating your thoughts frequently (assuming they're constructive) will win the respect of others, whereas supporting the view of the broader team (perhaps that of your boss) or remaining silent may be preferred in Korea, to portray your loyalty to the organization. To thrive in any setting, you thus need to familiarize yourself with the social and cultural norms.

LESSON 5

Do stretch yourself early

Son, as you start progressing through your career, you'll realize your roles and responsibilities change quite dramatically. For example, in investment banking, the new analyst may be responsible for financial modeling, taking notes, printing and bringing books to the meetings, etc. They are expected to be good at those and will be evaluated based on that. As they move up the ladder, an associate is expected to be able to quickly and accurately check the models that analysts have prepared, sometimes lead calls with clients, draft thoughtful presentations and more. As a VP or director, they are expected to supervise all the different workstreams, manage daily communication with clients, and maybe even bring in a few. A managing director's primary role is to win business and bring in revenue for the firm. Do you see how drastically things change from spending eighty percent of one's time in Excel and PowerPoint to eighty percent traveling and meeting clients? You must acknowledge and accept that to be successful in any organization.

If your feedback has been that you're technically very capable at the associate level, that's great. If that feedback persists as a director, then you're probably not focusing on the right area. Adapting yourself quickly to the changing roles isn't always easy, particularly if your responsibilities don't align with your personality. For example, if you're not outgoing and salesy, you'll find it difficult (though not impossible) to advance to managing director, as bringing in clients and winning business are the biggest criteria you'll be judged against. That's why you'll often be asked to, and you'll push yourself to get out of the comfort zone.

I myself have been fascinated and sometimes intimated, to be candid, by the added level of responsibility I was given over a short period of time—only a year or two into investment banking, I was leading calls with prospective buyers to discuss the unique market position and differentiated product offerings of the business we were selling. Moreover, I fielded questions from sophisticated private equity investors with respect to complex financial models and the granular assumptions that went into building the forecast. Nowadays, as a senior vice president, I frequently present my thoughts in front of the CEOs, CFOs, and sometimes the Board of Directors of large companies to help them make appropriate financial decisions. All these changes in responsibilities happened fast (in the matter of a handful of years), and I expect this pace to continue in the foreseeable future.

So, I encourage you to learn to stretch yourself early on and never be complacent. The best place to practice this is in schools, and that's why they're there in the first place. Find/explore what you like and practice what you aren't comfortable doing. If you are afraid of public speaking, do that in front of a classroom as often as you can. It'll save you a few embarrassing moments in front of your colleagues later on in life. If you're bad with numbers but still want to get into finance, take as many finance-related courses as possible and try out for internships. Schools are what I call "safe zones" in the sense that no one really judges you and the repercussions of making mistakes are minimal relative to the business world. So, utilize them as much as possible and experiment. Expose yourself to different groups of people and activities to uncover your strengths, weaknesses, and preferences. Finding what you want to do in life is the single most important, yet difficult assignment you're tasked with in life, so I encourage you to begin your quest as early as possible. Practice is key to confidence and success, and always remember that even the greatest basketball player in the history of the sport, Michael Jordan, spent a hundred hours a week on the basketball court.

LESSON 6

Do think in terms of your values

Son, when you're facing a challenging situation, think before you act or speak. There are going to be times when you're judged unfairly, provoked and/or insulted, among other things. You are free to respond (or not respond) in any way, but thinking before responding typically helps. So how should you think? Think in terms of your values, whatever they may be. For me, it's being fair, respectful, and helpful to others. So, when someone confronts me, I ask myself whether the response I plan to give is fair, respectful, and/or helpful to the situation? If it is, then I respond as such; if it isn't, then I'll rethink or maybe even decide not to respond at all. It's hard to be respectful to someone who mistreats you and I don't blame you if emotions come into play here. But constantly remind yourself of your values and have them be the principles that guide you through conflicts. Trust me, you'll feel great about yourself in the end.

Don't think things over multiple times, though. It's fine to sleep on an issue and think things through in the morning but recognize that overthinking may worsen things by putting unnecessary stress and anxiety on you, which are top ingredients for health issues. And time is priceless, so don't waste it on overthinking—it's simply not worth it. Just trust yourself and go with your values. If things don't turn out the way you would have liked them to, it's fine—you'll at least have the comfort in knowing that you've lived by your standards. And living by them is something that few people do, so you should be proud of that.

It's funny how I've lived a part of my life in anxiety, in things that have never happened, yet I have spent so much time thinking about them. For example, I was extremely anxious when I applied to business schools, agonizing over what I would do if I weren't accepted to any. Everyone around me advised that I relax a bit and pointed me to what I already had—a nice consulting job at a prestigious firm with enormous support from the partners. So, in retrospect, it wasn't that bad at all! The time I had wasted thinking through what an embarrassment I'd be if not accepted was a complete waste of time. What I should have done was acknowledge and appreciate that I had given it my best, and that's what's important in life regardless of the outcome.

With respect to what your values should be and how to form them, as aforementioned, mine are being fair, respectful, and helpful to others, while constantly looking for ways to learn and improve myself. These are just my set of values, and I don't believe there's a silver bullet when it comes to identifying the correct set of values for anyone (nor do I think it's useful) as one's experiences and observations largely shape them. What you should know, however, is that they're formed throughout life, they change over time as you expose yourself to different things and people, and that living by the values you define is difficult yet extremely rewarding. I advise you to read as many self-development books as possible and, perhaps as a starting point, digest Ralph Waldo Emerson's definition of success —"To laugh often and much; to win the respect of intelligent people and the affection of children; to earn the appreciation of honest critics and to endure the betrayal of false friends. To appreciate beauty; to find the best in others; to leave the world a bit better whether by a healthy child, a garden patch, or a redeemed social condition; to know that even one life has breathed easier because you have lived. This is to have succeeded." The last phrase, to know that even one life has breathed easier because you have lived, has had an evergreen impact on shaping my values and how I see the world. What reading books of well-established thought leaders allows you to do is to continuously develop and refine your views on values and appreciate the personal improvements and realizations that come along with it.

If you face an issue and have thought it through but just can't get the ends to meet, know that your mom and I will always be there for you to talk to. We will point you in the right direction or at least attempt to do so in the best possible way.

LESSON 7

Do exercise prudence

Son, as you get into the age of falling in love and others feeling emotions for you, you will be hurt, cry over breakups, and sometimes be full of joy. Life is that way, sometimes you don't get what you want, but other times you do. You can feel free to spend time with anyone that you're attracted to, though when it comes to marriage, exercise prudence. I suggest you find someone who you're most comfortable with. Someone who accepts your true self and vice versa. It's almost like finding the right roommate in college, the only difference being that you'll be living with that person for the rest of your life (or that's the plan at least).

Look at your partner's background, where and how she grew up. I only say this because it'll help determine what similarities you'll share and what challenges you may expect to face. Education is less important than passion—if she didn't go through the traditional education system, look at what she's passionate about and what she values, and what actions she has taken to pursue those. Passion, attitude, and perseverance will determine one's path, not necessarily an advanced degree. I neglected to say that her relationship with her parents is important and I did that deliberately. I've seen multiple people in rough relationships with their parents be extremely successful in their careers and families. Wanting to prove their parents wrong or be the exact opposite of their parents may have driven that. In any case, what I do encourage you to look at is the relationship *between* her mom and her dad. She grew up observing how they treat each other, so she has naturally absorbed those traits as the norm and may even have developed expectations (knowingly or unknowingly) on what kind of a husband she wants. It's the difference between expectations and reality that creates conflicts in a relationship. Knowing her expectations and norms will help you understand her better and ultimately make the right decisions.

For example, your mother's parents have lived quite a different lifestyle than my parents, primarily due to both of her parents working versus my father being the sole breadwinner in my household. Housekeeping efforts, such as preparing the meals, raising the children, cleaning the apartment, etc., were all equally divided up among her parents, while most of those tasks landed on my mother given her role as a housewife. Your mother's parents seem to be more of equal footing when it comes to making important family decisions, such as sending their children abroad for education, while I must say that my father typically called the shots. Having been raised in such different environments and parenting styles, your mother and I often got into arguments during the first few months of our marriage as to who does what and who ultimately makes decisions. Fortunately, these conflicts resolved themselves as we began to understand each other (and the backgrounds we'd been raised in) better, though the observations that we made in our childhood clearly do seem to influence and shape our thinking, behavior, and expectations of one another.

You'll obviously want to find someone you're physically attracted to. But remember that we age, and outward appearances change. Inner character, however, rarely does. Keep that in mind and don't solely go after the prom queen. I thought your mom was attractive when we were dating, but the more I get to know her, the more beautiful she has become in my eyes.

If you're in doubt about a person or a relationship, look at your mother and how she behaves and how she treats me/you. While your mother and I are by no means perfect beings, and neither is our relationship, you'll at least be able to pick up what you like (or can bear) versus what you don't like (or can't bear). Judge your relationship on how comfortable you are with that person, what she's passionate about, what values you have in common, and what her expectations and standards of a family are. Acknowledge the imperfections in her (and yourself) and see if you can live with them. I deal a lot with numbers so like to have everything planned and measured—your mother, who tends to be a bit more leaned back and spontaneous, has accepted that trait of mine even though it irritates her sometimes.

LESSON 8

Do select your friends

Son, forming friendships is important and an integral part of our lives. We are all social animals that desire a sense of belonging and can't live on our own. But remember to befriend those that truly want what's best for you. As you grow up, you'll be surrounded by people that don't always want that—they may be extremely selfish, may solely be attracted to you by the car you're driving, may just want your time and presence because they're bored, and so forth. I acknowledge the fact that humans are selfish by nature, but remember that our time on this planet is limited, and we all die. Do you want to spend time with someone who merely operates in their self-interest and doesn't even know (or care to know) what's best for you?

Friends come and go as you live through life, and your encounters with them tend to naturally decline as you form a family and commit to raising children. The ones that stick around and that you keep in touch with should be the ones you truly care about and vice versa. Jim Rohn, a successful entrepreneur, once said that you're the average of the five people you spend the most time with. If you're spending your time with people that you don't like, don't share similar values as you, and whose actions and thoughts irritate you, what does that reveal about yourself? Friends are there to share your happiness, to lean on when sad, to ease the pain, to laugh together, to discuss and debate the things you have in mind, to provide a different perspective, and to guide you along the way. I personally appreciate a friend that tells me I have salad in my teeth than those that refrain from doing so, but that's just my personal preference. When a true friend asks for help, be there for them. You will regret it if you decide to neglect them, and by the time you've found time to help that person, they may not need it. And trust me, there aren't going to be that many times when friends seek your assistance.

What I'm not intending to say is that you interact solely with your circle of friends. You could have collectively formed norms that are only applicable to your group of friends with similar backgrounds and beliefs, thus obscuring the perspectives of others dissimilar from you. Acknowledge that your standards (and those of your closest friends) aren't necessarily what others have in common nor what's right or appropriate for everyone. Spending time with those of different backgrounds and cultures mitigates the risk of you falling into the bias trap and broadens your views. And you don't have to commit endless hours nor be friends with them. It's interesting to me to see how often the words "different" and "wrong" are misused in Korean. "Different" is "da-reun" in Korean, but even native speakers frequently use "teul-lin" (which means to be "wrong") when referring to "different." In a country like Korea, where the individual is considered less important than the broader society, perhaps being "different" is perceived as "wrong" and thus the words are used interchangeably.

Have the end in mind as you form and foster friendships. When asked what people in their deathbeds regretted the most, the top responses included that they've spent too much time around toxic people but not enough time with friends and family. Moreover, many were extremely remorseful and ashamed that they hadn't given as much as they had taken. Live a life that's most fulfilling, without regrets but with joy and confidence that you've lived life at your best.

Don't—What You Shouldn't Be Doing

LESSON 9

Don't just listen

Son, someone once came into a public restroom in New York City and complained vigorously to himself that it stank. And I thought to myself, isn't this place supposed to stink? It's fine to emit gas in a restroom, but that obviously isn't the case in a conference room full of people. The difference between the two is the setting and audience —you're meant to take care of business in a conference room, and you're meant to clean up after yourself privately in a restroom. Said differently, you're fine to do certain things under a specific setting and audience, which may not be the case in another. So, read the setting and audience as you enter any room to define what's appropriate and what isn't.

This principle applies to the business world as well. Let's say you are an investment banker advising your client on an offer they have received to sell the company. You're asked to present your views on the potential sale in front of the Board. You may find the CEO to have a totally different set of interests than a Board member. The CEO may be much more emotionally attached to the company, given his thirty-plus years of tenure with the business so unwilling to sell at this point. The Board member, on the other hand, may want what's best for the shareholders of the company so they may solely focus on the offer price and terms. You're now faced with two somewhat opposing sets of interests and if you haven't identified them well in advance of the meeting, it'll be difficult for you to set the tone and effectively deliver the message. What complicates things is the fact that people typically don't reveal their true interest, especially if it is personal or opposes the broader interest of the group. Moreover, a Board usually consists of multiple constituents and each individual may have their own sets of interests.

This begs the question—how can you identify the different sets of interests of the audience? I first advise you to learn the difference between a *position* and an *interest*. Let's follow the previous example. The CEO is unwilling to engage the buyer, noting that the offer isn't attractive and that the buyer is financially unstable. Those are *positions* that the CEO has taken. The *interest* is the motive behind why he's acting the way he does. Again, he may be emotionally attached to the company as he founded the business thirty years ago and doesn't want to lose control of it. He may think he'll never be appointed the combined company's CEO and doesn't want to report to anyone else, recruit for another job, or retire yet. He may believe the financial package he'll receive from the M&A transaction won't be attractive or that his salary may go down. Or his interests may be a combination of all the above. Whatever his interests are, you need to see beyond his position to be able to pinpoint where he's coming from. This will allow you to be in a much more comfortable position to select your tone and negotiate regardless of the setting. It turned out that the CEO didn't want to lose the control and autonomy he had to run the business when the merger occurred. Once his interests became apparent, we worked with the buyer and came up with a solution, offering him a Board seat at the combined company along with continued duties to run his business as a separate entity. The buyer also effectively raised his level of responsibility, as he was now tasked with overseeing and supervising certain divisions/geographies of the buying entity and was responsible for spearheading the execution of the joint synergy plans. If we hadn't uncovered the CEO's true interests, the negotiation process and merger itself might have been severely delayed or even stalled. The only way to influence others is to get them what they truly want or show them how to get there. Knowing the interests of others thus empowers you to influence them, allowing each individual to get a step closer to their desired outcomes.

We say in investment banking that a mandate is won well in advance of the actual pitch. What that means is that the banker has spent enough time with the key constituents to get to know their interests before delivering the presentation to the broader group. I want you to get into the habit of identifying the true interests of others. Build trust, ask the right set of questions, perhaps in a discrete setting, and truly try to think from the other person's perspective. Map out the various parties involved and write down your views of their potential interests to see the big picture. And don't forget to identify who the key decision-makers are.

LESSON 10

Don't let money be your goal

Son, we live in the center of capitalism, New York City, and are perhaps led by one of the most profit-oriented Presidents in the history of the United States. I've witnessed people throwing others under the bus, so they stand out and are lavishly compensated. I've dined with people that each spent over a thousand dollars for a wine-paired course meal at Eleven Madison Park, where just across the street, two ladies were picking out empty cans and bottles from filthy trash bags for five-cent refunds. I know of individuals that fly on their private jets to rest in their mansion in Nantucket, Massachusetts every weekend of the summer while discussing the $1,500 haircut they've gotten last week, which surprisingly doesn't look too different from the one they had previously gotten. They're oftentimes surrounded by flamboyant women rocking Chanel heels topped by the limited-edition Hermes Birkin bags and Van Cleef necklaces. So, it isn't too difficult to see what money can bring someone, is it?

Money can buy materialistic things from extravagant cars to luxurious vacations. It provides financial stability and mental comfort, especially when faced with adverse events, such as being fired or getting ill. You can build your own business and experiment around without having to worry about getting that paycheck. Money can get the attention of others and sometimes even attract people, though know that if they're only drawn to you by your wealth, they won't stick with you if you lose the money.

So, what is it that money can't get for you? True love and friendship are things that money can't buy. It can't get you inner joy and sometimes even deliver the opposite if you're too obsessed with it. I know a few incredibly rich individuals who are too afraid of losing their wealth and constantly compare themselves to those that have accumulated more than they have. A 2010 Princeton University study found that there is a strong correlation between money and happiness to the point of $75,000 of annual income, but it vanishes above the $75,000 mark. I think it's because there are only certain things you can do at any given moment in time—a limited number of meals you'll eat a day, a limited number of places you can be in a day even if you own multiple houses, etc. Once you've met your essentials for living, the law of diminishing returns dictates that more money doesn't necessarily translate into more happiness.

I want you to use money as a tool to accomplish your goals and not have money be your ultimate goal in life. If your goal is to have a happy family with kids when you're thirty, use the money to invest in financial assets to secure the down payment needed for the house. You may also use it to buy those books on parenting and continue to educate yourself on how to successfully raise children. Or use the money to pursue an advanced degree for a financially rewarding job to support your family. Whatever choices you make with your money, I encourage you to use it to accomplish your goals. That will reveal the true value of money and provide you with a sense of achievement and success. If money is your ultimate goal in life, you'll find yourself never having enough.

I fully understand you want to look good in front of others, dress nicely, eat delicious meals and so on. Feel free to do so responsibly, when you have "sufficient" money. "Sufficient," in my view, means that your decisions to spend on certain things don't adversely and dramatically impact your well-being elsewhere—e.g., if you choose to buy a leather jacket for two thousand dollars and lose the ability to buy textbooks for classes, you're out of your mind. On the other hand, if you're living a frugal life despite having enough money and a real necessity to spend it somewhere, you're also not doing the right thing. So, it all has to do with spending responsibly and to a degree where your spending pattern doesn't result in losses or suffering in other essential parts of your life. Distinguishing what's needed (your "essentials") from what's wanted (your "luxuries") and prioritizing spending on the essentials is wise. Showing off your money, whether you have it or not, just by virtue of being recognized is silly.

As embarrassing as it may sound to you, I myself have shown off money in the past. Back in my junior year of college, I purchased a used Mercedes Benz C230 Coupe. Customary to many coupes and Mercedes' standards, it was a rear-wheel drive, which meant that it would often slip on icy roads. I was in Madison, Wisconsin for undergrad, where it snowed almost half the year, so you can only imagine the practicality of owning a C-Class Coupe. Your grandparents had given me somewhere around $20,000 to purchase a safe vehicle in consideration of the weather conditions, probably never expecting me to buy a used, rear-wheel drive 2-door coupe. I think they still don't know of it. In any event, I couldn't buy a new Mercedes for $20,000, but I was able to purchase a used C-Class that I thought would impress people. It was by no means practical and I recall having to sometimes even take my friends' cars to get somewhere because it wasn't drivable in severe snow. And being a used car, I did run into quite a few costly maintenance issues as well, such as tire misalignments. So, did I end up impressing others? I don't think so because not many people even remember me owning the C-Class as it was mostly parked in my garage. Did I end up selling the vehicle at a reasonable price when I graduated? No, I think I sold it for a bit over $14,000 after merely a year or so of driving it, because not many people in Wisconsin are looking for a coupe. So, did I ultimately regret having spent $6,000 plus all the maintenance charges for a year of driving, or more like nine months of driving and three months in the garage? Yes, absolutely, but I now think of it as the price I paid to learn that showing off money simply doesn't bring the value that you think it will.

LESSON 11

Don't let others define your worth

Son, I want you to live a life that's full of joy. The harsh truth, however, is that pain and suffering are inevitable. In order to minimize suffering, you must learn to remove dependencies on others. If you're happy because someone smiled at you, you're dependent on that person. If you feel valued only when your followers like your Instagram post, you're dependent on your followers. Early in your life, you'll depend on us to take care of you—to provide food, a comfortable place to sleep, to change diapers, etc.—and that's absolutely normal. As you grow up, though, you should detach yourself from your dependencies so that the source of happiness is you versus others. Isn't it sad to see how many people determine their worth by the attention they receive from others, including ones they don't even know personally?

The world has evolved to a place where you can see the gorgeous lives of others in a split second by scrolling down on your phone. The attention that some people seek on social media and their addiction/dependency on it seems ludicrous to me. Posting a picture of your lavish vacation or high-end car only generates more likes and followers, so people thrive for that. But what happens if they don't receive the attention anymore? They feel worthless, lost, and eager to post more.

This is a modern conundrum that technology has cast on us. As I've outlined in Lesson 7—"Do exercise prudence," the difference between *expectations* and *reality* is what creates tension. The bigger the gap between the two, the less happy you will be. You inevitably set your *expectations* by what you see on social media and compare them to the *reality* you're living in, only to become ashamed of your circumstances and surroundings. What you should instead be doing is comparing yourself to who you were yesterday and not to someone else. I've stopped being on social media and it has helped me tremendously. I now don't waste time determining which pictures to upload, what filters to apply, and how to best position them. Said differently, I've deliberately detached myself from impressing others and measuring my self-worth based on what they think of me. It has certainly been a gratifying experience.

I was recently watching a show on Netflix, where a five-year-old YouTuber making millions of dollars was asked by her mother what she wants in life. Her response was just so mindboggling that I can't forget—she said she wants more money. Seeking money isn't the issue here; what frightens me is the fact that the YouTuber is only five years old—is that the right value to have as a child? And what happens if her sources of happiness—fame and money—suddenly vanish?

I acknowledge being popular and receiving attention from others can often seem rewarding, especially when you're young. But remember that if your self-worth is largely determined by someone else's perception of you, then you really can't live a life full of happiness. The source of joy should be you. Your values and not someone else's should determine your self-worth. So, if your value is to continuously improve and give it your best all the time, then you should measure yourself against those principles versus someone else's perception of you. What matters to someone on their deathbed is not the attention they have received from others they don't know, but the lack of attention they've given to those that they do know and care about.

LESSON 12

Don't find rich friends

Son, as you become of age, you'll soon realize that life isn't fair. You're dealt with a set of cards that differs from others. You'll sometimes appreciate the quality and abundance of things you have, but human nature frequently dictates that we compare ourselves to the ones who have more than we do. You may ask things like, why am I not taller, why is he so much faster than me, why can't we live in an eight-bedroom mansion, and so forth. Genetics make up a large part of our current being, and the mansion may simply just be out of our league financially. Realize that those are the cards you've been dealt with and that it's hard (if not impossible) to change any of it. Complaining over something that you don't have will never make you happy.

A very wealthy friend of mine once told me that, among the many reasons he gives to charity, one might be because he's tired of comparing himself to even wealthier people. As I've noted previously, humans tend to look up and compare themselves to those that have more versus less. So, giving to the less wealthy allows him to see and appreciate what he has versus what's missing. As the Dalai Lama famously says in his book *The Book of Joy: Lasting Happiness in a Changing World*: "If you want to be poor, find some rich friends; if you want to be rich, find some poor friends."

I was once driving a car on a sunny summer day back in 2012. Stopped at the traffic light, I looked to the side to see a tiny old Kia with its windows down. Inside of it, a young couple was holding hands with the woman leaning against the man as if he were her only spinal cord. I have never witnessed a smile that portrayed so much happiness to date and immediately made a note to myself —"For some, a small rusty Kia may not even be a car. Others will appreciate just having any vehicle for use. For some, a supermodel in her early twenties may just be a pain in the butt. Others may consider an annoying girlfriend their supermodel. After all, it all boils down to the rather epic question, whether the glass is half full or half empty."

Look at the brighter side of things and appreciate what you have. Many times, I find that we long for the things that we don't have, simply because those aren't in our possession. A few years ago, I really wanted a Rolex, so I spent a significant amount of time researching the different models, price points, dealerships, and so forth. It was exciting in many ways as I got to learn about the different types of watches that were out there, what was popular, what watch experts say about resale value, where and how I should make the purchase to get the best pricing, and so forth. After I had finally purchased the Rolex four months later, my appreciation of it merely lasted a week, realizing that I had longed for something simply because it wasn't in my possession. Once you finally have what you have longed for, you may find it isn't as rewarding as you thought it'd be.

LESSON 13

Don't be on my side

Son, as of writing this book, I've known your mom for fifteen years, and we're approaching our fourth anniversary. Customary to many couples, we've had our ups-and-downs, including our share of arguments. In the unfortunate event that we argue in front of you, please be on your mom's side even if you think I'm right. What the years of marriage have taught me is that women tend to be more emotional and seek sympathy. Just acknowledging the struggles she's going through will make her feel better and often resolve the issue. I wouldn't want to imagine the emotional stress and sadness she'll feel if you were to take my side when we argue.

A friend of mine has spent several thousand dollars on marriage counseling. He told me about an incident where his wife was sick, so he laid her down, fed the children, and played with them until they fell asleep. He ran several restaurants by himself, so he was tired after getting back home but didn't express any frustration as he acknowledged raising the children was part of his duties as well. Despite his efforts, he continued to get into arguments with his wife and eventually decided to get counseling as he couldn't understand what he was doing wrong. After several sessions and a few thousand dollars later, the counselor's remarks that struck him the most were that all his actions were effectively meaningless unless he sympathized with her. So, all his efforts playing with the three children, feeding them, doing the dishes and whatnot were things that she appreciated, yet what she sought after most was a warm set of words of sympathy.

In Korea, there's a saying that you can pay off a million-dollar debt with just words. Have sympathy towards your mother and express that. I will try my best on any occasion as well.

LESSON 14

Don't take anything for granted

Son, you must acknowledge that Christine is not only your mom but my wife as well. We put a lot of thought into having a child and take full responsibility for you—nothing changes that. But remember that she has been my wife many years before you were even born, and I truly love her. I frequently run into couples that sacrifice everything for their children. They take out a sizable loan to send their children to private schools, move to a place where commute to work is horrible, but their children benefit from a better education system, live an extremely frugal life only to feed their children organic foods, etc. I won't get into whether those parenting styles are good or bad as everyone's values and circumstances differ, though I encourage you to acknowledge and appreciate whatever sacrifices your mother and I have made for having and raising you.

My mentor often reminded me of an old Korean saying—if favors persist, people take them for granted and conceive them as their rights. A friend of mine kept asking his parents to look after his daughter throughout the week so he could run errands, meet friends, work out, etc. His parents loved seeing their granddaughter so continued that for almost two years, at which point, they began having health issues and couldn't accommodate the baby anymore. My friend was frustrated with his parents' reluctance and argued with them as to why they wouldn't be willing to take care of their own granddaughter. To him, the sacrifices that his parents had continued to make for a couple years weren't something that he appreciated but only took for granted. Instead of thinking about how he'd return the favor, he openly expressed anger and disappointment towards his parents. See how a favor persisting over time can disguise itself as a privilege? Recognize the sacrifices that others make and express gratitude. Gratitude allows you to see from the perspective of others, reminds you to be respectful, and eventually makes you happier.

If you feel comfortable being around someone, whether a friend, loved one, colleague, or whomever, it might simply be the case that you're both wired the same way as one another. However, it might also mean that someone has continued to make sacrifices that the other person may be unaware of to keep up the relationship. In many cases, it's a mix of the two, but I want you to acknowledge and appreciate the sacrifices that others have made, which oftentimes don't vividly appear on the surface at first glance and are overlooked. Show gratitude towards those that make you feel good and comfortable. Be specific and sincere when showing your appreciation as that will get into the hearts of others and be remembered. And don't forget to apologize when you realize you've made a mistake. The following quote is what has intrigued and enlightened me about the intent of apologizing—"Apologizing doesn't always mean you're wrong and the other person is right. It just means you value your relationship more than your ego."

I mentioned to you earlier that Christine has been my wife since before she became your mom. I said it because I honestly am not sure how well I would be able to tolerate it if you were to take her sacrifices and favors for granted. As her husband, it is my duty to make sure she is well. I recognize that we're mostly on the receiving side of things as children. When you become of age, though, I want you to see what others have given you, not because we want anything in return but because I want you to get into the habit of practicing gratitude.

LESSON 15

Don't neglect your health

Son, we only live once, and the cards are dealt as soon as we're born. You can't be someone else, but I trust you want to be the best version of yourself. To accomplish that, good health is a prerequisite—you'll find it extremely difficult to reach your full potential and become the best version of yourself if you have serious health issues.

I've encountered several people who had everything in life that one could imagine, but when faced with a serious illness, they only wished they could give up everything in return for their health, regretting they hadn't taken care of themselves earlier on. Wealth, status, and all other accomplishments are meaningless if you're constantly lying in a hospital bed with multiple IV injections running through your veins. Good health comes from our genetic makeup, nutrition, exercise, and peaceful mind. You can't control genes since you're born with them, but you can control nutrition, exercise, and to a certain extent, your mind.

The things I'll mention are incredibly cliché, but at the same time, I would be remiss if I didn't include them on my list because of their significance in life. Eat properly and a variety of different foods. Exercise consistently and at least three times a week, mixing up the routine with cardio and weight training. Think positively and practice gratitude to ease your mind and minimize stress. Stress is harmful to both your mind and body, deteriorating even the healthiest people alive. Your mom joined several running clubs, runs races in Central Park and Brooklyn, and is participating in the upcoming NYC half marathon this March. I'm less of a cardio guy but enjoy lifting weights—my body fat was slightly north of 12% earlier this year when I had my medical checkup. Though I haven't been able to hit the gym lately, I know I feel so much better (both mentally and physically) when I work out consistently. You'll not only sleep better but also become more energetic and confident in yourself.

You may believe you're born healthy and that the benefits of regular exercise and a clean diet are trivial to you, but I want you to remember, the time and effort you put in today will shape your wellbeing a few years from now. And the health you think you're born with probably is a result of good eating and exercise habits in the past. So be consistent in your workout and diet. I recognize it takes commitment to exercise and eat healthily, but nothing meaningful in life comes without some form of suffering. Leverage the abundance of media outlets available to you for a nutritious diet, productive exercise, and a clear mind. Your mother and I will act as proxies for living a healthy life.

LESSON 16

Don't expect others to change

Son, I've only lived thirty-six years, but I'm fascinated by the changes that have occurred in my time. When I was in elementary school, cell phones were practically nonexistent. But when you look around now, by the time someone gets into middle school they may have already gone through a couple different iterations of the iPhone. Your grandparents' TV was so large and boxy that I thought I could fit my aquarium in it, but now you can see those flat screens attached to walls and some will even bend? Not too long ago, I recall waiting thirty or more minutes for a taxi to come by, but nowadays people have access to a myriad of ride-hailing services on their six-inch cell phone. And about a year ago, CNBC was discussing which company would be first to become $1 trillion in market capitalization and look where Apple is trading today ($1.36 trillion).

These are changes primarily driven by technology, but social norms change too. Back in the '80s, I was hard-pressed to see a couple of the same gender in public. You'll see for yourself if that's the case when walking around New York City today. When your grandparents got married, your grandmother gave up her work instantly and lived with your grandfather and his parents for several years before moving out. Now there are so many couples that make a living together and residing with one's parents is simply not the norm. When my aunt was in college, she was arrested for publicly speaking ill of the Korean President; now, political satire is prevalent in all forms of media.

But if you believe that individuals change, think again. A grown-up's mind has already fully established its standards and boundaries, so it's highly unlikely that they will change. Needless to say, it's even harder if someone were to force the change. In my experience, when I wanted to change the thinking or behavior of someone, it usually meant that I cared for that person. If I didn't, why would I want to change that person in the first place? So, my point is this—you must accept the people around you the way they are. Even if you care for someone and truly mean it for their best, don't force and expect them to change. Their "best" may differ from yours, depending on their background, beliefs, circumstances, etc. I once saw a Facebook post from a friend of mine, questioning the motives of someone who had disrespected him when all he was trying to do is help that person. The comment that had the most thumbs-up was—they never asked for it.

The Serenity Prayer has stuck on to me for years and I'm hoping it serves you as a guidepost as well—"God, grant me the serenity to accept the things I cannot change, courage to change the things I can, and wisdom to know the difference." While I still struggle to sometimes tell the difference between what I can versus can't change, your mom and I acknowledge you're your own being and promise to encourage and comfort you, but never steer in a certain direction.

www.ingramcontent.com/pod-product-compliance
Lightning Source LLC
Chambersburg PA
CBHW062124220526
45471CB00010B/3873